CONCERT FAVORITES

Volume 2

Band Arrangements Correlated with
Essential Elements Band Method Book 1

Page	Title	C___	Correlated with Essential Elements
2	Bandroom Boogie	Michael Sweeney	Book 1, page 11
3	Beethoven's Ninth	arr. Paul Lavender	Book 1, page 11
4	Gallant March	Michael Sweeney	Book 1, page 11
5	High Adventure	Paul Lavender	Book 1, page 11
6	Rock & Roll—Part II (The Hey Song)	arr. Paul Lavender	Book 1, page 11
7	Amazing Grace	arr. Paul Lavender	Book 1, page 24
8	Infinity (Concert March)	James Curnow	Book 1, page 24
9	Latin Fire	John Higgins	Book 1, page 24
10	Linus and Lucy	arr. Michael Sweeney	Book 1, page 24
11	Theme from "Star Trek® Generations"	arr. Michael Sweeney	Book 1, page 24
12	American Spirit March	John Higgins	Book 1, page 34
13	Gathering In The Glen	Michael Sweeney	Book 1, page 34
14	The Loco-Motion	arr. John Higgins	Book 1, page 34
15	Royal Fireworks Music	arr. Michael Sweeney	Book 1, page 34
16	Scarborough Fair	arr. John Moss	Book 1, page 34

ISBN 978-1-4234-0076-9

HAL•LEONARD®
7777 W. BLUEMOUND RD. P.O. BOX 13819 MILWAUKEE, WI 53213

00860164

BANDROOM BOOGIE

B♭ CLARINET

MICHAEL SWEENEY

00860164

2

BEETHOVEN'S NINTH

B♭ CLARINET

LUDWIG VAN BEETHOVEN
Arranged by PAUL LAVENDER

00860164

GALLANT MARCH

Bb CLARINET

MICHAEL SWEENEY

00860164

HIGH ADVENTURE

Bb CLARINET

PAUL LAVENDER

00860164

ROCK & ROLL – Part II
(The Hey Song)

Bb **CLARINET**

Words and Music by
MIKE LEANDER and GARY GLITTER
Arranged by PAUL LAVENDER

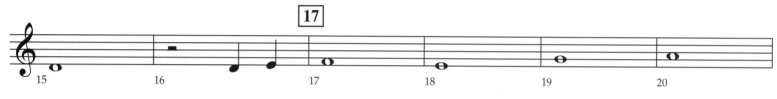

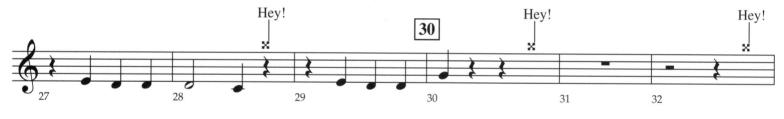

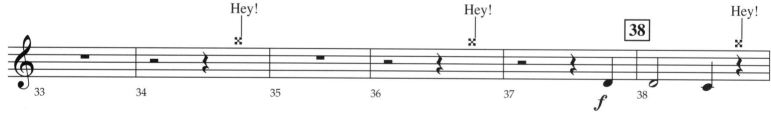

00860164

AMAZING GRACE

Bb Clarinet

Traditional American Melody
Arranged by PAUL LAVENDER

INFINITY
(Concert March)

B♭ CLARINET

JAMES CURNOW (ASCAP)

00860164

LATIN FIRE

JOHN HIGGINS

Bb CLARINET

LINUS AND LUCY

Bb Clarinet

By VINCE GUARALDI
Arranged by MICHAEL SWEENEY

(From The Paramount Motion Picture STAR TREK GENERATIONS)
THEME FROM "STAR TREK® GENERATIONS"

Bb Clarinet

Music by DENNIS McCARTHY
Arranged by MICHAEL SWEENEY

00860164

AMERICAN SPIRIT MARCH

B♭ CLARINET

JOHN HIGGINS

GATHERING IN THE GLEN

B♭ CLARINET

MICHAEL SWEENEY

00860164

THE LOCO-MOTION

Bb CLARINET

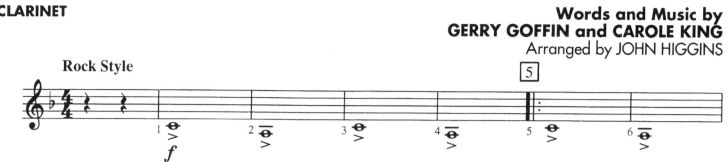

Words and Music by
GERRY GOFFIN and CAROLE KING
Arranged by JOHN HIGGINS

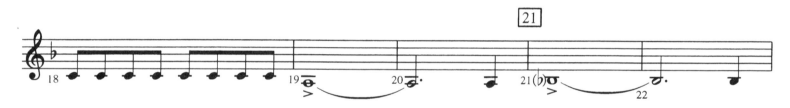

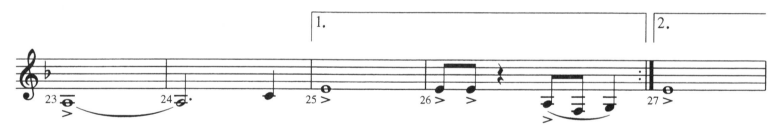

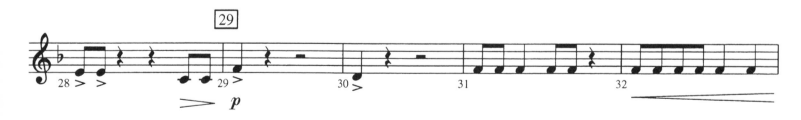

00860164

ROYAL FIREWORKS MUSIC

GEORGE FREDERIC HANDEL
Arranged by MICHAEL SWEENEY

B♭ CLARINET

00860164

SCARBOROUGH FAIR

B♭ CLARINET

Traditional English
Arranged by JOHN MOSS